WE'RE GOING CAMPING!

Written & Illustrated
By Patrick Bochnak

For my grandchildren,
Paige and Cooper
MY LITTLE HAPPY CAMPERS

WE'RE GOING CAMPING!

Written & Illustrated
By Patrick Bochnak

My sister and I saw our
dad out in the garage,
he was gathering camping
gear for a trip.
I hope it's like last year,
it was so much fun.

WE'RE HEADED ON AN ADVENTURE
BUT WE DON'T KNOW WHERE.
IT COULD BE THE MOUNTAINS,
OR MAYBE TO THE LAKE, IT
MIGHT BE THE OCEAN,
MOM AND DAD WON'T SAY.

CAMPIN
IDAHO

THERE ARE SO MANY
WAYS TO CAMP,
THIS PERSON HAS A
CAMPER ON HIS TRUCK.

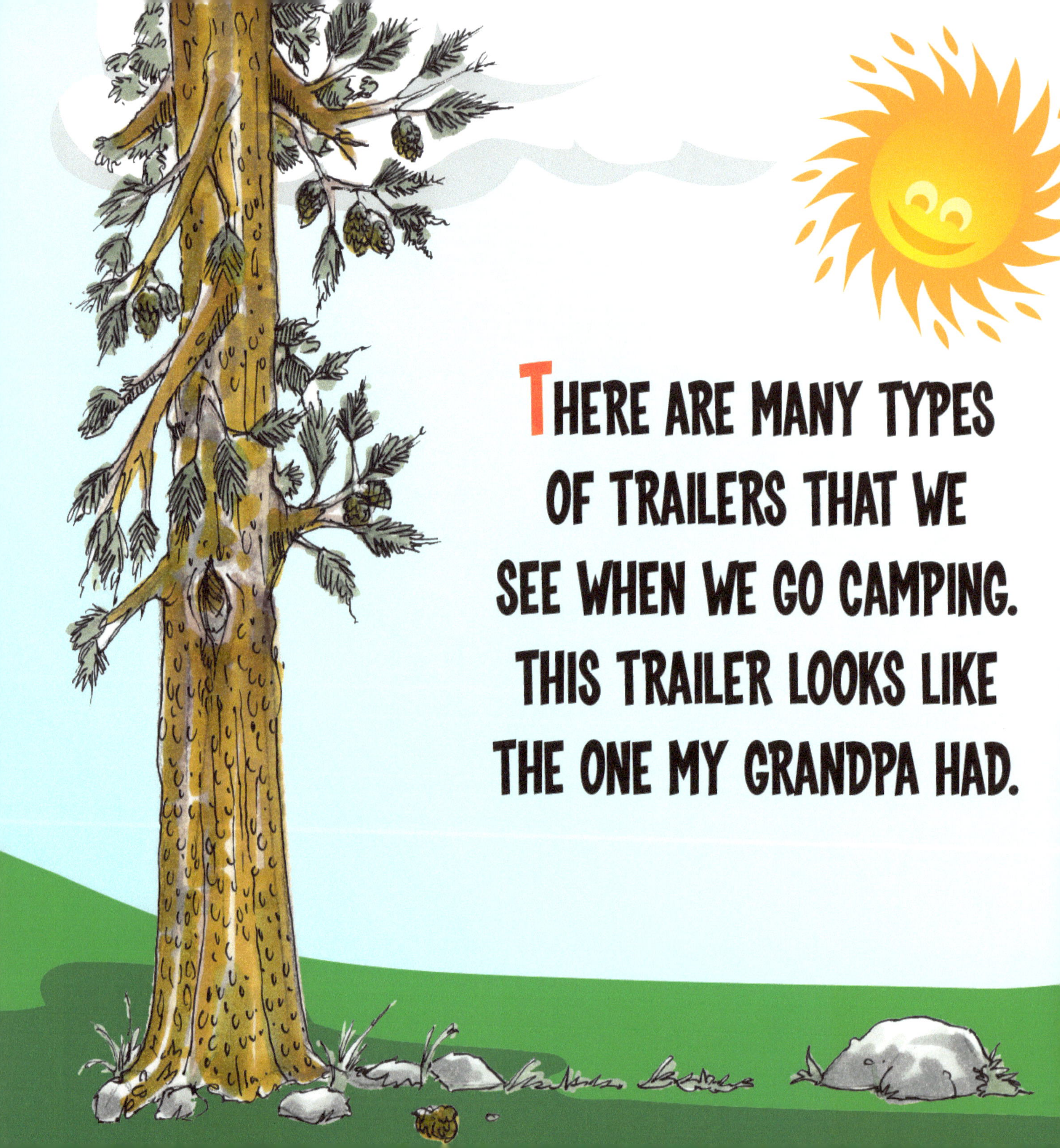

There are many types of trailers that we see when we go camping. This trailer looks like the one my grandpa had.

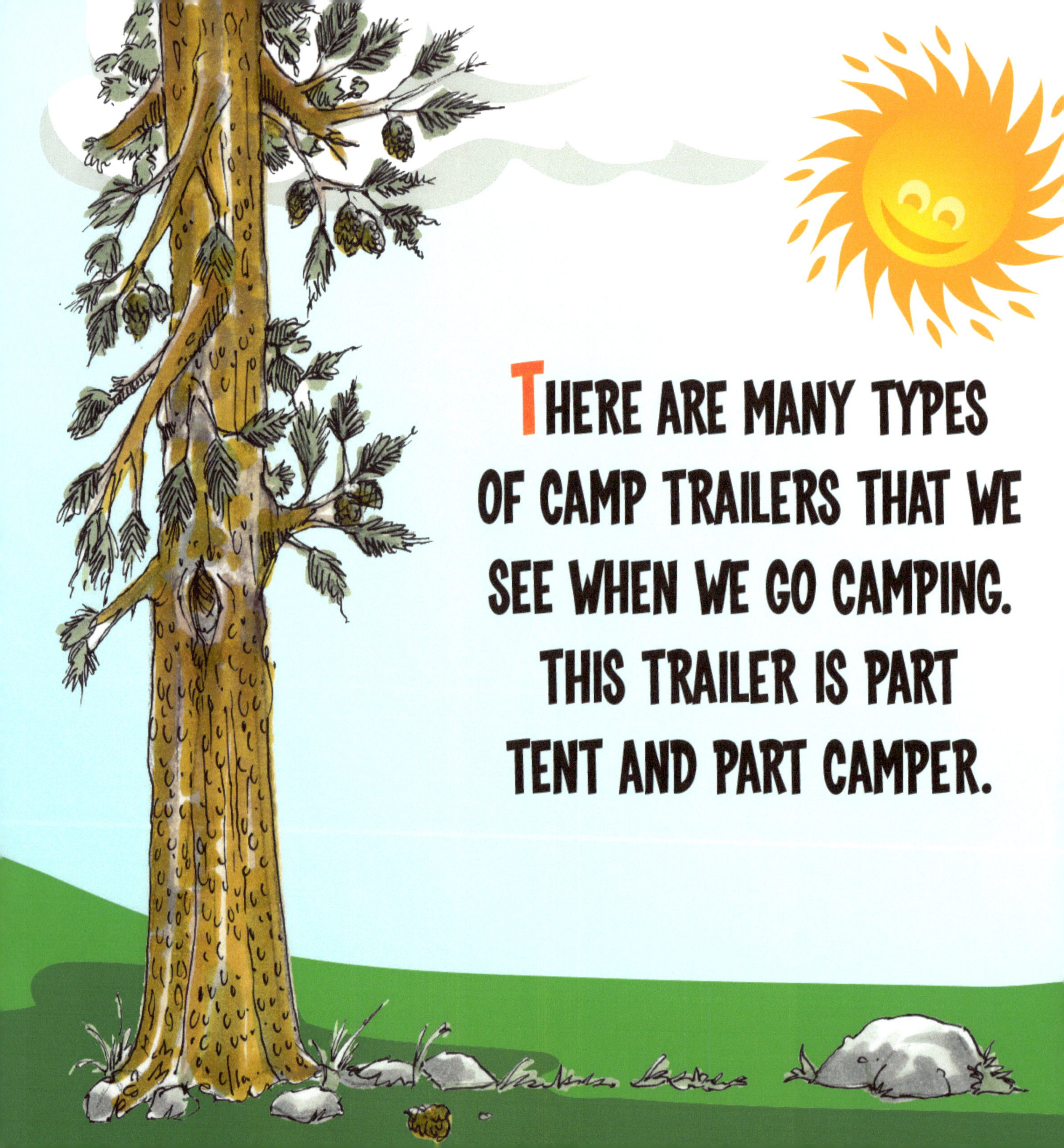

THERE ARE MANY TYPES OF CAMP TRAILERS THAT WE SEE WHEN WE GO CAMPING. THIS TRAILER IS PART TENT AND PART CAMPER.

There are many types of camp trailers that we see when we go camping. This camper looks like a spaceship from Mars.

SOME PEOPLE LIKE TO HIKE INTO THE MOUNTAINS. THEY CAMP IN A TENT BECAUSE IT'S EASY TO CARRY IN A BACKPACK.

When we camp near a river,
mom relaxes in a chair
while dad tries to catch a fish.
Sister and I dig in the sand
and make sand castles.

THE LAKE IS SO MUCH FUN TO FLOAT ON. WE ONLY GO IF WE HAVE OUR LIFE VESTS ON, AND THE WATER IS CALM. OUR PARENTS ARE ALWAYS WATCHING US.

ON HOT DAYS WHILE CAMPING,
DAD LIKES TO SIT IN HIS
OLD TUBE ON THE WATER
AS LONG AS HE CAN.

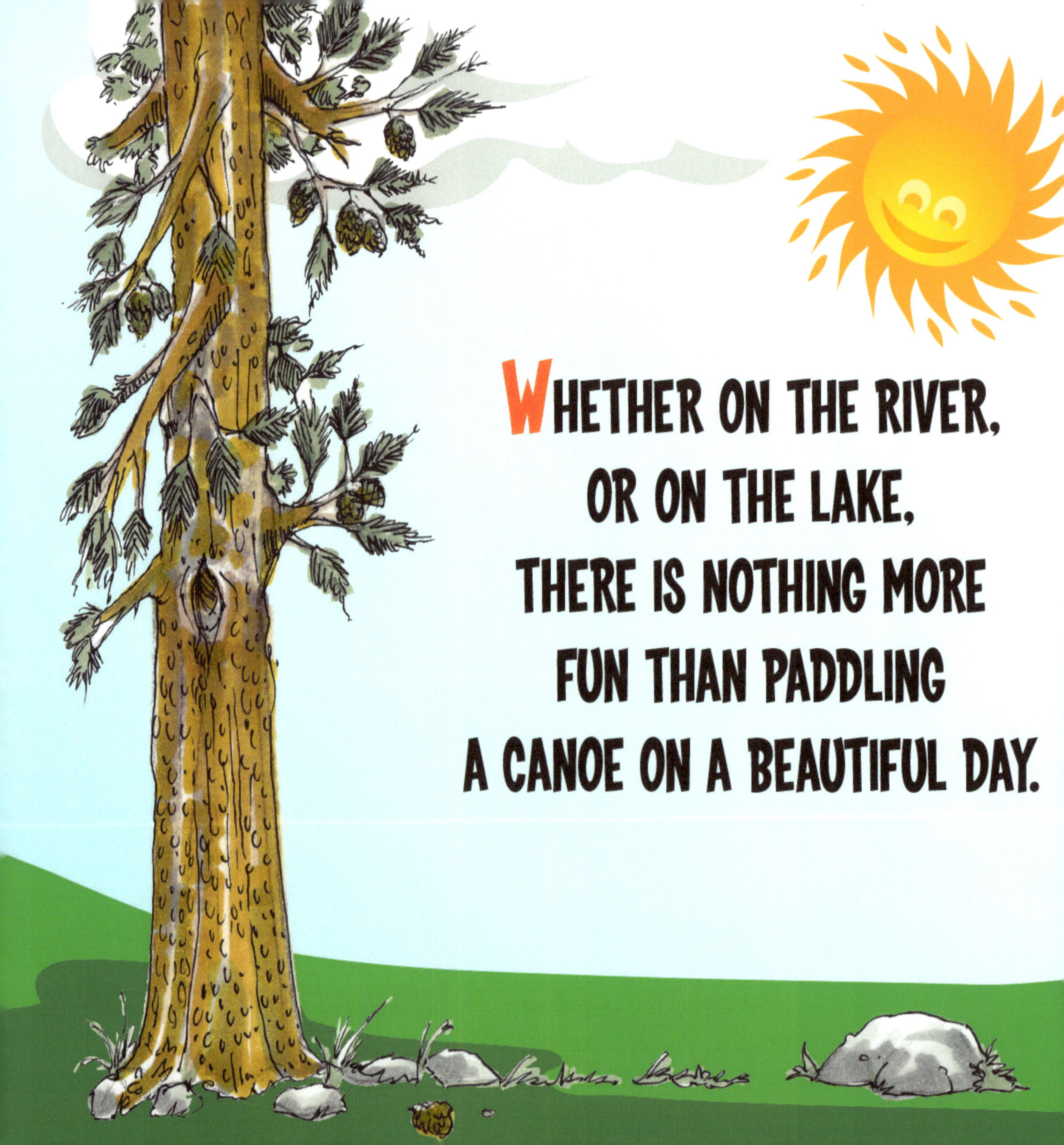
WHETHER ON THE RIVER,
OR ON THE LAKE,
THERE IS NOTHING MORE
FUN THAN PADDLING
A CANOE ON A BEAUTIFUL DAY.

Dad and I love
spending time together
fishing on the lake,
and sometimes we fish
in the river.

WHEN WE GO CAMPING, MY SISTERS ALWAYS MAKE SURE THAT THE VOLLEYBALL NET, AND BALL GET PACKED FOR THE TRIP.

WHEN WE GO CAMPING,
YOU CAN BET THAT
SOMEONE BROUGHT A GUITAR.
WE CAN ALL SING FUN
CAMPING SONGS TOGETHER.

SONGS

WHEN WE GO CAMPING WE LOOK FOR DIFFERENT KINDS OF BUGS. WE LIKE TO LEARN AS MUCH ABOUT THEM AS WE CAN.

When the sun starts to go down at the end of the day, some animals come out to run and play.

ROASTING MARSHMALLOWS ON A STICK IS A SPECIAL TIME MY MOTHER AND I LOVE TO SHARE.

UP IN THE MOUNTAINS FAR
FROM THE CITY LIGHTS,
THE NIGHT SKY IS BRIGHT.
YOU CAN CLEARLY SEE
FALLING STARS, AND SATELLITES
SHOOTING ACROSS THE SKY.

THE BEST PART OF CAMPING IS GETTING UP IN THE MORNING, AND HAVING DAD'S SUPER SPECIAL PANCAKES.

KISS
THE
COOK

WHEN WE GET READY TO LEAVE CAMP, MOM CLEANS THE TRAILER, BROTHER AND I PICK UP TRASH, AND DAD PUTS THE FIRE OUT. OUR CAMP SITE IS ALWAYS CLEANER THAN WHEN WE ARRIVED.

WATER

SMORE'S
A CAMPING TRADITION

BUILDING THE PERFECT SMORE.

NOW SQUISH IT ALL TOGETHER AND EAT IT.

WHEN YOU GO CAMPING IN THE WILD, YOU MAY SEE ANIMAL TRACKS ON THE GROUND OR NEAR THE WATERS EDGE. HERE ARE SOME TRACKS TO IDENTIFY.

SQUIRREL

Spanish (Ardilla)

CHIPMUNK

Spanish (Ardilla)

RACCOON

Spanish (Mapache)

FOX

Spanish (zorro)

DEER

Spanish (cierva)

ELK

Spanish (alce)

RABBIT

Spanish (conejo)

COYOTE

Spanish (Coyote)

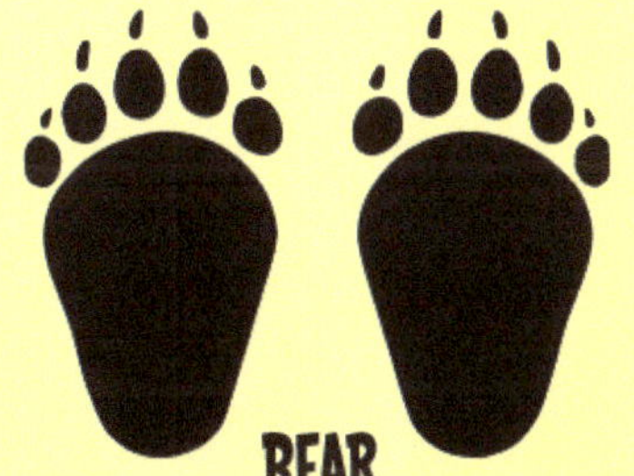

BEAR

Spanish (oso)

WOLF

Spanish (lobo)

BOBCAT

Spanish (gato montés)

BADGER

Spanish (tejón)

MY CAMPING ADVENTURE

Write down fun things to remember from your camping trip, or draw a picture.

MY CAMPING ADVENTURE

Write down fun things to remember from your camping trip, or draw a picture.

MY CAMPING ADVENTURE
Write down fun things to remember from your camping trip, or draw a picture.

MY CAMPING ADVENTURE
Write down fun things to remember from your camping trip, or draw a picture.

MY CAMPING ADVENTURE
Write down fun things to remember from your camping trip, or draw a picture.

About the author

Patrick Bochnak is an illustrator / cartoonist with a passion for writing and illustrating children's books. Patrick has been in the illustration and design field for over 25 years.

Patrick's stylistic illustrations and designs have been featured in books, news publications, posters, fliers and magazines for decades.

He was born and raised in Central California, spending many of his formative years living and working on cattle ranches. He discovered his love for art at a very young age. Patrick's idea of taking a reading test was drawing battle scenes instead of actually taking the test, thankfully he learned to read. When Patrick wasn't ,"being the explorer" hitchhiking across the country, riding bulls and climbing cliff faces in cowboy boots, he was studying design and illustration techniques in college.

Patrick resides in Kuna, Idaho with his wife, Cherie, and Jack the cat. He enjoys hunting, camping, playing guitar, antiquing and doing whatever his lovely wife commands. Patrick is a good hearted, down to earth country boy filled with love, humor and creativity.

Books By Patrick Bochnak

Children's Paperback Picture Books

The Great Potato Legacy Of Patty O'Malley

I Think There's a Monster in My Garden

Caterpillar

When We Were Young